Simple-to-Sew

APPLIQUÉ

APPLIQUÉ

Master new sewing skills with these
simple-to-make projects

HELEN MILOSAVLJEVICH

B T Batsford Limited, London

First published in Great Britain by B. T. Batsford Ltd.
4 Fitzhardinge Street, London W1H 0AH

ISBN 0-7134-7929-9

A catalogue record for this book is available from
the British Library

This book was designed and produced by
Quintet Publishing plc.
The Old Brewery
6 Blundell Street
London N7 9BH

Creative Director: Richard Dewing
Designer: Isobel Gillan
Project Editor: Anna Briffa
Editor: Lydia Darbyshire
Illustrator: Nicola Gregory
Photographer: Andrew Sydenham

Typeset in Great Britain by
Central Southern Typesetters, Eastbourne
Manufactured in Singapore by Eray Scan Pte. Ltd.
Printed in Singapore by Star Standard Industries Pte. Ltd.

ACKNOWLEDGEMENTS
The publisher would like to thank the following
for their help and advice on this title:
Elsa Godfrey; Creativity, Needlecraft Specialists,
45 New Oxford Street, London;
and The Quilt Room, 20 West Street, Dorking, Surrey.

CONTENTS

INTRODUCTION

Appliqué, in simplest terms, is the stitching of different fabrics to a background to create a decorative effect. The versatility of appliqué means that it can be suitable for wall-hangings and pictures, clothing and soft-furnishings of all types. The projects in this book will give you a sound basis for various appliqué techniques using hand and machine stitching with suggestions for equipment and materials, finishing techniques and how to design your own work. The projects range from the simple Pot Holder to the more complex Rainbow Trout Wall-hanging and are designed to extend your knowledge and improve your technique. They have been chosen to present as many different styles, methods and items as possible.

BASIC MATERIALS

Fabric

Many different types and weights of fabric can be used for appliqué, although it is a good idea to choose compatible weights for both appliqué and background in any one project. Cotton fabrics have been used for the projects in this book, and are highly recommendable since they are easy to cut and stitch, adhere well with bonding and are easy to launder. It is always advisable to wash all chosen fabrics before use to check for shrinkage and colour fastness.

Wadding

This is a fibrous material used as a filling between layers of fabric. It is available in polyester, silk and cotton, and is generally sold by weight per square yard/metre. It is usually washable and requires no special treatment, although some cotton wadding may need washing before use – always check the manufacturer's instructions. 2oz/50g polyester wadding is recommended as good, general, all-purpose wadding, since it is light and easy to stitch. Do not iron items once the wadding is in place, since it will lose its "springy" quality.

Interfacing

Fusible interfacing has been used for these projects. It has a double-sided adhesive web, bonded on one side to a paper backing. This allows accurately drawn motifs to be pressed onto fabrics before sewing by hand or machine. It is not necessary to leave a seam allowance since the bonding prevents the fabric from fraying.

To use, trace your motif onto the paper backing, remembering that the resulting image will be reversed. Press the non-paper side of the interfacing onto the wrong side of your fabric and cut out the motif, using the drawn outline as a guide. Carefully remove the paper backing from the motif, position the motif on your background fabric and iron into place.

Freezer paper

The use of freezer paper as an aid to appliqué is quite recent. It has a waxy surface on one side and plain paper on the other. Primarily it is used to ensure that the appliqué motif is kept as flat as possible while being hand stitched to the background fabric. To use, transfer your motif to the plain side of the freezer paper, remembering the resulting image will be reversed. Cut the motif out, and iron the paper, waxy side down to your fabric. Cut round this with a ¼–½in/5–10mm seam allowance, which is then clipped and pressed over the paper shape before stitching it to the background fabric. The paper can be removed through a gap left, and there is no sticky residue.

Freezer paper can also be used to prevent puckering and wrinkling when a motif is sewn to a background fabric by machine and satin stitch is used. Simply iron the waxy side of a suitably sized piece of freezer paper to the underside of the background fabric to correspond with the position of the motif. Then peel off once the piece is stitched in place.

A large part of the fun of appliqué lies in choosing matching and contrasting fabrics from the vast selections available.

BASIC EQUIPMENT

Sewing kit

A sewing kit with good quality tools is essential for all types of appliqué work. Equip yourself with the basics initially, and then add to your kit as you develop your skills and designs.

A basic sewing kit needs to consist of: dressmaking scissors, sharp-pointed embroidery scissors, general-purpose scissors, needles, pins, a wide range of all-purpose threads, suitable for hand and machine sewing, fabric marker, thimble, tape measure and unpicker/seam ripper.

Other items that you may wish to add are pinking shears for decorative edges, beeswax to strengthen the thread for hand quilting, and a rotary cutter which offers greater accuracy when cutting fabric.

Your basic sewing kit need not be expensive, and is essential in order to produce professional-looking work.

Frames

Small appliqué projects do not generally require the use of a frame. However, using an embroidery frame can result in a better finish, since the fabric is kept taut, and allows for more accurate stitching. An embroidery frame can also be used for machine appliqué if the presser foot is removed and the feed dog dropped to allow for free-style embroidery. Practice is essential for good results.

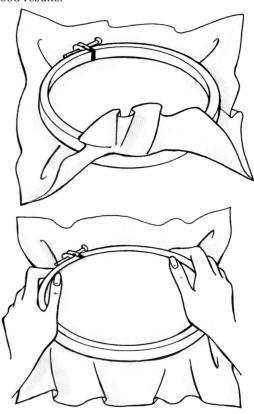

Hoops come in a wide range of sizes, and all work on the same principle as the one above.

Quilting frames can be bought in many shapes and sizes, generally larger than hand-held embroidery frames, and often free-standing, leaving both hands free for stitching.

BASIC TECHNIQUES

Hand stitching

The Turned Edge Method is always used when applying motifs by hand. Once your motif is in position on the background fabric, it can be pinned and basted. Then it can be stitched neatly in place with small stitches, always ensuring that the seam allowance is turned under with your fingers or the needle as you go.

Machine stitching

Generally motifs are applied by machine using satin stitch. This is a very dense zigzag stitch, usually used for buttonholes. You will need to set the right length and width of stitch before starting, and you may wish to practise on scrap material first.

It may help to keep your motif in place using interfacing or freezer paper (see page 7).

Begin stitching at the edge of the motif and continue slowly and smoothly around the shape. Keep the needle in the fabric when changing direction, and finish off by leaving long threads which you then pull through to the wrong side and fasten off by tying together.

Bias strips

The true bias of any fabric is always at a 45 degree angle to the selvedge.

To make bias strips from a square of material using the selvedge as a guide, you need to fold the material diagonally and press the fold. Mark strips of an equal width parallel to the fold, open the fabric and cut these strips. (Remember to leave a seam allowance on both edges of the strip.)

If you have no selvedge to act as a guide, you will need to establish the grain of the fabric, then measure and cut a square. Then you can proceed as before.

If the strips need to be joined, place one strip on top of another at right angles to each other with the right sides together, and stitch across the diagonal join.

Bias tubes

They are used quite often in appliqué and can be made quite easily. Firstly you need to measure and cut a strip of binding which is twice the required width, plus ¼in/5mm seam allowance on both edges. Fold the strip in half lengthways, right sides together and stitch. It is not necessary to turn the tube to the right side, but it can be pressed with the seam in the centre, hiding the raw edges.

It may help to have a press bar for this purpose. This is a precut length of heat resistant plastic which can be bought in varying widths. It is inserted into the tube and ensures that the seam is centred accurately.

TEMPLATES

Accuracy is important when making templates in order to achieve good shapes for appliqué work. All measurements for these projects are given in both imperial and metric. It is important that you stick to one or other for any one project, since the conversions are not compatible.

When it comes to cutting the template out, use a craft knife or good quality paper-cutting scissors. You should never use dressmaking scissors for cutting card or paper.

To make templates

1 Trace the motif using a sharp pencil and either tracing paper or template plastic. The templates need to be very accurate and have no seam allowance added. Template plastic is useful as its transparency allows the selective placement of the template onto patterned fabric.

2 The motif may need to be enlarged. Use graph paper or a photocopier and follow the scale given.

3 Cut out the motif and, if using tracing paper, glue to firm card, remembering to reverse the image if required to for the project.

4 Write any particular instructions on the template – direction of grain, number of motifs to be cut, etc.

5 Place the template onto the right side of the fabric, aligning the grain of the fabric with your line on the template. The grain of your motif should run the same way as on the background fabric.

6 Draw around the template with a marker pen or pencil and cut out with a seam allowance of ¼in/5mm.

A sharp pencil and good ruler are essential for template-making. Graph paper can be used to enlarge or reduce the sizes of a template, and template plastic is useful for the more accurate placing of motifs on fabrics.

APPLIQUÉ TECHNIQUES

Persian appliqué

This technique involves cutting out motifs from patterned fabrics, which are then reassembled into a new design. Motifs from several different fabrics can be used, generally on a plain background for a more striking effect.

Shadow appliqué

Transparent layers of fabric such as muslin, voile and organza can be overlaid on bright colours, to produce a more subdued effect. The appliqué motifs are arranged on the background, before being covered. Careful stitching around the motif, usually by hand, ensures that it is firmly held between the layers. Embroidery on the transparent fabric can be added if extra embellishment is required.

Padded appliqué

Appliqué shapes can be padded in order to give the illusion of being larger and more rounded. Wadding or toy stuffing is used, and can be inserted either through a gap left in the stitching before the shape is completely applied, or by making a cut in the wrong side of the fabric, behind the applied shape, which is then oversewn after stuffing.

Hawaiian appliqué

Originating in Hawaii, this technique traditionally involves just one single motif being applied to a background fabric. The motif is initially cut from a piece of paper that has been folded into quarters and then eighths, and which is then attached to fabric folded in exactly the same way. This is then cut out, and the result is a symmetrical shape with 4 or 8 points. This is then applied, by hand, using the turned edge method. Striking two-colour combinations are particularly effective using this method.

Ribbon appliqué

This is an effective and decorative way of applying fabrics to a background, and the variety of ribbons, lace, braids and broderie anglaise available is extensive. They can be applied either flat or preformed as bows and rosettes, or can be used to form decorative patterns or highlight specific areas of design.

Designing your own work

Designing something that will be enjoyable to create and which will give pleasure once finished can involve a lot of planning and preparation. It is advisable to keep a design simple when aiming to create an effective example of the technique chosen, and to avoid being too ambitious, aiming to complete your work within a reasonable timescale. Colour, shape and texture are of primary importance for your design, and inspirations may come from a great many sources – items at home, holiday souvenirs, pictures from books and magazines to name but a few.

Always look for strong, well-defined shapes which will translate easily into a flat design. Plan your ideas on paper using a geometry set if you have one. Trace shapes from pictures, and simplify them if necessary. Look at fabrics available and be inspired by the patterns, shapes and colours.

Once you have decided on the technique and size of your finished item, draw your design to actual size, making templates for it if required, and calculate the amount of material you will need. Then you can cut out your shapes and arrange them on a background fabric, until you have an arrangement that you are happy with.

HAWAIIAN APPLIQUÉ CUSHION

Finished size: 18 x 18in/46 x 46cm

This cushion, which is made from medium weight cotton fabric, is decorated with a striking motif that is cut from a single piece of fabric and applied to the background fabric by hand. The vivid greens look bright and summery, and the cushion would be perfect in a conservatory or sunny breakfast room.

Copy the template (see page 45) and transfer it to the card. The outline given represents one-quarter of the finished shape.

YOU WILL NEED

- card for template
- patterned fabric: 11 x 11in/28 x 28cm
- cream fabric: 1 piece 14 x 14in/ 36 x 36cm; 2 pieces, each 20 x 12in/ 51 x 30cm
- needles, sewing thread to match, scissors, pins
- plain green fabric: 2 pieces, each 14 x 3in/ 36 x 7.5cm; 2 pieces, each 20 x 3in/ 51 x 7.5cm
- muslin: 20 x 20in/51 x 51cm
- lightweight polyester wadding: 20 x 20in/ 51 x 51cm
- quilting thread

1 Fold the square of patterned fabric in half, then in half again. Press with an iron and pin to hold the layers together. Place the template on the fabric, matching the edges of the template with the folds of the fabric. Hold it firmly and draw around the template. Remove the template and cut out the motif through all four layers of fabric. Remove the pins, open out the motif and press it lightly.

2 Take the square of cream fabric and fold it diagonally into quarters. Press it lightly with an iron and open it out.

3 Place the motif on the cream fabric, using the creases to position the motif symmetrically. Pin the motif in place then baste it so that the line of stitches is about ⅜in/8mm from the edge of the motif.

4 Use matching thread to slip stitch the motif to the cream fabric, turning under the raw edge with your needle as you work. Clip the concave curves so that they lie smoothly, and remove the basting.

5 With right sides facing, pin and baste the two short strips of plain green to opposite sides of the cream square. Stitch, leaving a seam allowance of ¼in/5mm. Press the seams together and outwards.

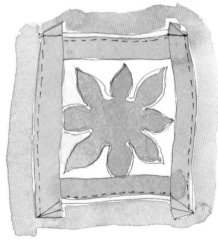

6 Repeat with the two longer strips on the two remaining sides, stitching across the ends of the shorter strips as well as across the cream square. Remove pins and basting.

7 Place the muslin, wadding and cushion top on your work surface.

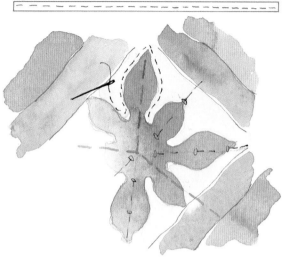

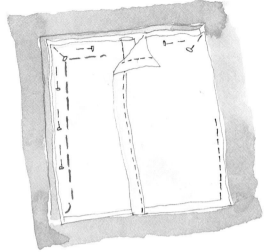

9 Use quilting thread and a small running stitch to quilt a line all around the motif, about ¼in/5mm from the edge of the patterned fabric. If you wish, add more quilting lines. Remove pins and basting.

10 Take the two cream rectangles and turn in a hem of about ½in/10mm on one of the long edges of each piece. Lay the two pieces, right sides facing, over the cushion front. The pieces will overlap in the centre. Pin and baste, then stitch around all four edges. Clip the corners, remove pins and basting and turn to the right side before inserting a cushion pad.

8 Beginning in the centre and working outwards in all directions, pin and baste the layers together.

STAR PAN HOLDER

Finished size: 7 x 7in/19 x 19cm

The simple four-pointed star is pieced together from diamonds made with a paper base. The star is then applied by hand to the front of the pan holder, and a layer of wadding between the back and front provides protection from hot handles and dishes. Medium weight cotton fabric is used throughout.

YOU WILL NEED

- card and brown paper for templates
- small pieces of patterned fabric, at least 4 x 4in/10 x 10cm
- needles, sewing thread to match, scissors, pins
- plain fabric: 2 squares, each 7 x 7in/ 19 x 19cm
- fabric for edging, 2½in/6cm wide: 2 pieces, each 7in/19cm long; 1 piece 8in/20.5cm long; 1 piece 11½in/29cm long
- lightweight polyester wadding: 7 x 7in/ 19 x 19cm

Trace the diamonds (see page 45) and make templates for the paper and fabric. Use the smaller diamond to cut four diamonds from the brown paper. Use the larger shape for the card template, which includes a seam allowance of ¼in/5mm on all sides, to draw diamonds on the patterned fabrics.

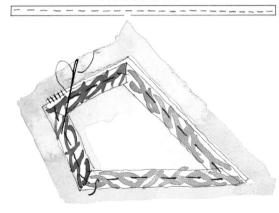

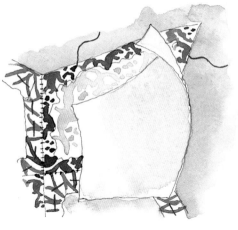

1 Cut out the four diamonds from the fabric. Place a paper diamond on the wrong side of each fabric diamond and pin it in place.

Fold the seam allowance firmly down over the paper, starting at the base of the diamond. Tie a knot in a length of basting thread and baste the paper and fabric together. Stitch right around each diamond, taking special care at the points to mitre the fold so that the fabric forms a neat angle.

3 Take two adjacent diamonds and, right sides facing, carefully oversew along one short edge. Take care to match the centre points and try not to stitch through the paper. Repeat with the two remaining diamonds.

5 Carefully remove the basting thread from around each diamond and ease out the paper. Press and baste the free edges down again.

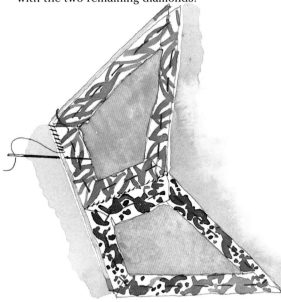

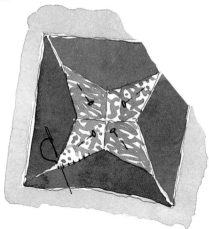

2 Press each diamond under a hot iron and then place them on a flat surface so that they form a star.

4 Complete the star shape by placing the diamonds together, right sides facing, and oversewing along the centre line. Take great care to align the centre point.

6 Take one of the large squares and fold it in half diagonally, then again into quarters. Press it and unfold it. Place the star shape on top, right side up, and align the points of the star with the creases, making sure that the star is equidistant from the corners.

Pin and baste the star in position. Using matching thread, carefully oversew around the edge of the star, finishing off on the wrong side. Remove all pins and basting stitches, then press.

Take the folded edging strip that is 8in/20.5cm long and place it, raw edges together, along the front edge of one of the remaining sides. Allow ½in/10mm overlap on each end of strip. Pin, baste and stitch in place. Turn over the strip to the back, turn in the ends at the corners and oversew them neatly before hemming the edge of the back.

7 Sandwich the wadding between the two squares of fabric. Pin and baste together. Take the strips of edging fabric and fold each in half lengthways with wrong sides together, ironing them in place. Place one of the short strips, raw edges together, along one edge of the fabric and wadding. Pin and baste, then stitch down, leaving a seam allowance of ¼in/5mm.

10 Make a loop by stitching the free end of the binding strip securely to the back of the edging. Remove all pins and basting stitches.
If you wish, quilt by stitching along the outside shape of the star.

8 Fold over the strip to the back of the square and hem down. Repeat on the opposite side.

9 Place the remaining strip along the fourth side so that it overlaps by about ½in/10mm at one end and 4in/10cm at the other. Pin, baste and stitch in place along the front edge of the square. Turn in the short end and oversew to form a neat corner. Turn over the strip to the back of the square and hem it in place, oversewing the edges of the unattached length together and turning in the end to neaten.

TABLE MAT

Finished size: 11½ x 14½in/29 x 36cm

The machine quilted gingham table mat looks fresh and bright with its large appliqué apple. The apple, which is stitched by hand, is shaped on freezer paper, which gives a smooth, wrinkle-free finish. Cotton wadding is used to give a firm base for the quilting, and medium weight cotton fabric is used for the mat and for the apple.

YOU WILL NEED

- card for templates
- freezer paper
- red cotton: 6 x 6in/15 x 15cm
- green cotton: 6 x 6in/15 x 15cm
- cotton wadding: 11½ x 14½in/29 x 36cm
- gingham fabric: 1 piece 11½ x 14½in/ 29 x 36cm; 1 piece 13 x 16in/33 x 40cm
- needles, sewing thread to match, scissors, pins

Use the outlines on page 45 to make templates for the apple and leaves. Reverse the templates and draw around them onto the paper side (not the waxy side) of the freezer paper.

Cut out the shapes and iron the waxy side of the apple to the reverse of the red fabric, and the leaves to the reverse of the green fabric. Cut out the apple and the leaves, leaving an allowance of ⅜in/10mm all round each shape.

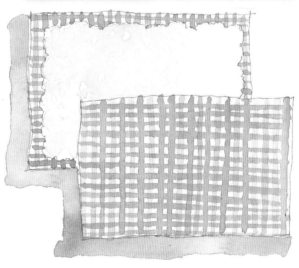

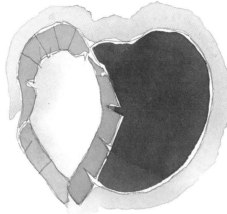

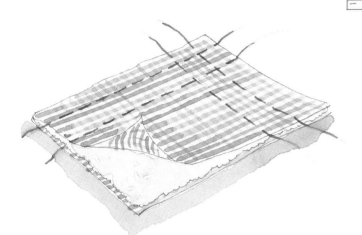

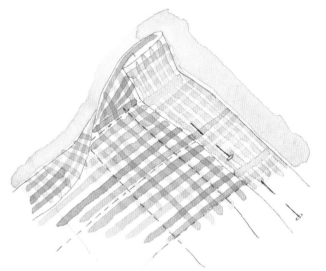

1 Place the wadding centrally on the larger piece of gingham, and lay the smaller piece of gingham so that it exactly covers the wadding. Pin and baste the layers together, making sure that they are held by vertical and horizontal rows of stitches at intervals of 4in/10cm.

3 Use sharp scissors to make a series of snips, about ½in/10mm apart, around the shape, taking care not to cut too close to the freezer paper. Press the allowance over the paper to form a smooth, neat edge.

5 Turn in the side edges of the bottom layer of gingham, folding them twice to create a hem about ½in/10mm deep that covers the raw edges of the wadding and the top layer of gingham. Pin and baste in place, then machine stitch along the edge of each hem.

Repeat the process along the two long edges, making sure that the corners are square. Remove all pins and basting stitches.

4 Position the apple on the mat, pinning and basting it in place. Slip stitch around the apple, leaving a gap of about 1½in/4cm.

Remove the pins and basting stitches and ease the paper through the gap, if necessary using a round-ended knife to release it from the fabric. Fold the edge under to keep the apple in shape and close the gap. Repeat with the leaves.

Use a sewing-machine to satin stitch the stem or embroider it by hand. Press lightly if necessary.

2 Using the gingham squares as a guide, quilt the mat by machine stitching vertical and horizontal lines, spaced at intervals of 10 squares or 1½in/4cm. Remove pins and basting.

CAFETIÈRE COVER

Finished size: 13in/33cm

Keep your coffee hot with this stylish cafetière cover. The striped medium weight cotton is firmly machine quilted so that it will withstand frequent laundering and so that it does not puff out between the letters, which are formed from bias strips and applied by hand.

YOU WILL NEED

- striped fabric: 1 piece 13½ x 20½in/ 35 x 52cm; 1 bias strip 1½ x 20in/ 4 x 51cm (join 2 pieces if necessary)
- card for template
- needles, sewing thread to match, scissors, pins
- lining fabric: 13½ x 20½in/35 x 52cm
- lightweight polyester wadding: 13½ x 20½in/35 x 52cm
- contrasting fabric: about 9 x 36in/23 x 90cm for bias strips; 1 x 4in/2.5 x 10cm (not on bias)

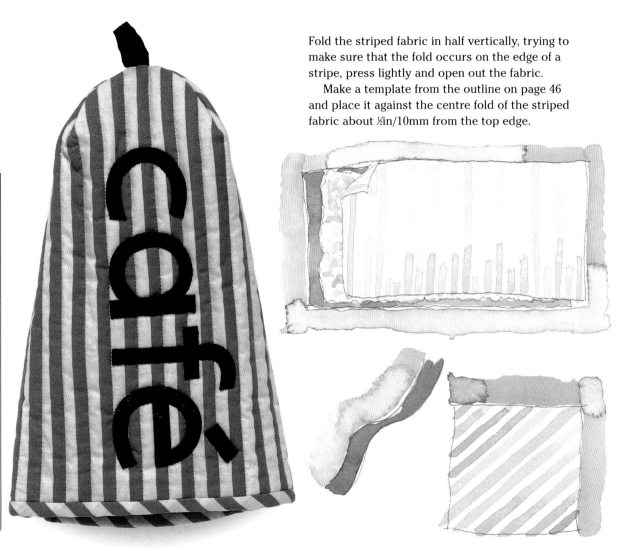

Fold the striped fabric in half vertically, trying to make sure that the fold occurs on the edge of a stripe, press lightly and open out the fabric.

Make a template from the outline on page 46 and place it against the centre fold of the striped fabric about ½in/10mm from the top edge.

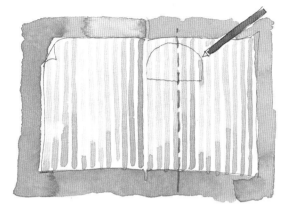

1 Draw around the outline with a pencil or marker pen. Use a contrasting colour of cotton to baste a vertical line of stitches from the apex of the arch to the bottom edge of the fabric and baste a second, horizontal row, across the lowest points of the curve. These lines are to help you position the lettering.

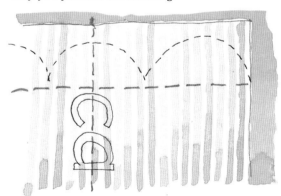

2 Draw around the template three more times across the fabric and stay stitch around the top curves. Trace the letters for "café" (see page 46) and transfer them to the fabric, positioning them sideways and using the basting stitches as a guide so that the curve of the "c" just touches the horizontal line and the vertical line passes through the centres of the letters.

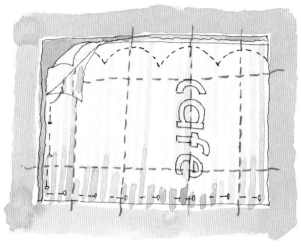

3 Lay the lining material, wrong side up, on your working surface, place the wadding on top of it and place the striped fabric, right side up, on the wadding. Pin and baste the layers together, with both horizontal and vertical lines of stitches, which should be about 4in/10cm apart.

Use your sewing-machine to quilt the layered fabric, stitching in vertical lines and using the stripes as a guide. The quilting lines should be no more than ⅝in/15mm apart. Take out the pins and basting stitches.

4 Prepare bias strips 1¼in/3cm wide, for the letters (see page 8) and, with wrong sides together, fold each in half lengthways. Stitch ¼in/5mm in from the raw edges and trim the raw edge carefully. Press the tube so that the seam is central when the tube is flattened and begin to apply the letters, starting with the "c".

Baste both sides of each letter in place before slip stitching it down firmly. The raw ends of all the letters should be turned under to give a neat finish, but the ends of the curved section of the "a" and the straight cross piece of the "e" can be left because they will be covered by the other pieces of the letters.

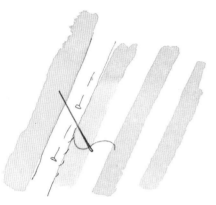

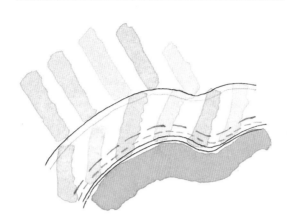

5 Cut around the arch shapes, about ¼in/5mm from the stay stitches, then, with right sides together and the curves matching, pin and baste the short edges together to form a tube. Leave a generous allowance and stitch the seam. Remove the pins and basting stitches, then carefully trim one side of the lining, wadding and striped fabric to about ¼in/5mm from the seam and the striped fabric and wadding of the other side. Fold the remaining lining over the trimmed edges, turn in the raw edge and baste then slip stitch the turned edge to the lining.

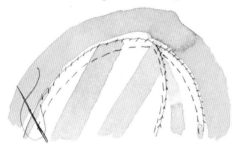

6 With right sides facing and working clockwise, match adjacent curves, pinning and basting before stitching from the base of each curve to the centre top, with a seam allowance of about ¼in/5mm. Neaten the seams by oversewing and fasten off securely in the centre.

7 Turn to the right side and, with right sides facing, place the bias strip of striped fabric around the bottom of the cover, beginning at the side seam and allowing about ½in/10mm turn-in. Baste and stitch in place. Remove the basting stitches and turn the strip up to the inside of the cover. Turn in the raw edge by about ¼in/5mm and slip stitch into place.

8 Take the small piece of contrasting fabric and stitch it, with right sides facing, to form a tube. Turn to the right side and fold in the ends by about ¼in/5mm to neaten. Join the ends to form a loop and attach it securely to the centre top of the cover.

GARDENING APRON

Finished size: 16½ x 16½in/31 x 31cm

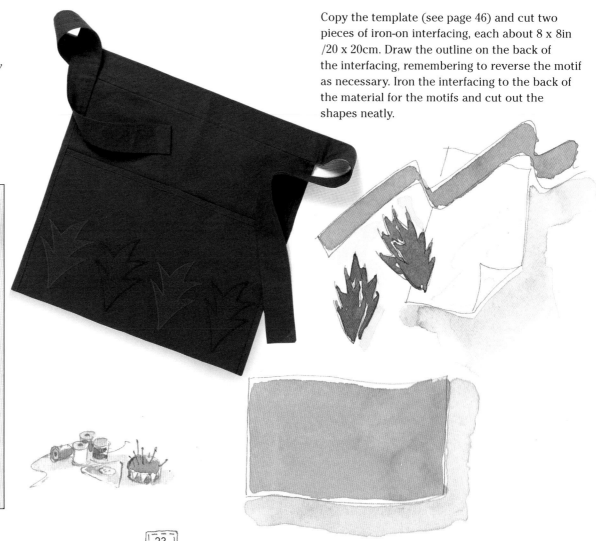

This useful apron is ideal for gardening – the deep pockets are large enough for packets of seeds and balls of twine and all those other small items that seem to go astray just when you need them. The apron is made from hard-wearing and practical gabardine, and the long ties make it easy to fasten. The motifs are applied to the front with a sewing-machine.

Copy the template (see page 46) and cut two pieces of iron-on interfacing, each about 8 x 8in /20 x 20cm. Draw the outline on the back of the interfacing, remembering to reverse the motif as necessary. Iron the interfacing to the back of the material for the motifs and cut out the shapes neatly.

YOU WILL NEED

- card for templates
- fusible interfacing
- gabardine: 1 piece 18 x 26in/46 x 66cm; 1 piece 60 x 5in/150 x 13cm (join 2 pieces together if necessary)
- needles, sewing thread to match, scissors, pins
- medium weight cotton for motifs: 2 pieces, each about 8 x 8in/20 x 20cm
- contrasting thread for appliqué

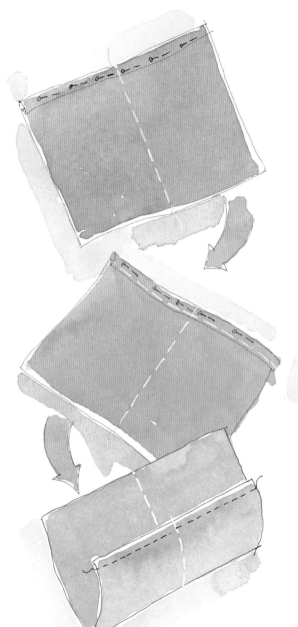

1 Take the large rectangle of gabardine and fold it in half lengthways. Press and run a line of basting stitches along the crease. Open out the material. Turn over one of the short edges by about ¼in/5mm, then turn this amount over again to create a hem. Pin and baste, press it, then top stitch with a medium length machine stitch.

Measure 10in/25cm from the hemmed edge, with the stitched edge outwards, and fold the fabric back. Press along this fold, which will become the bottom of the apron, and mark the fold with a line of basting stitches.

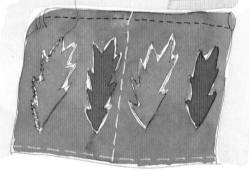

2 Remove the backing paper from one motif and place it on the front section of the apron – that is, with the hemmed edge facing – about 1½in/4cm in from one side and 1in/2.5cm up from what will be the bottom edge. Iron the motif in place then use the satin stitch setting on your machine and a suitable thread to stitch around the motif (see page 8). Make sure that the stitches cover all raw edges.

Apply the second motif – we alternated the colours – making sure it aligns with the first. Apply the third and fourth motifs, aligning them at the base and spacing them evenly across the gabardine so that the fourth one is about 1½in/4cm in from the other side. Press.

3 Fold the apron along the line of basting stitches at the bottom of the apron so that the motifs are facing outwards. Pin and baste the side edges together and pin and baste the central line along the basting stitches made in step 1. Turn in the side edges by ½in/10mm and then by the same amount again to form a neat hem. Pin, baste, then, with a medium setting, machine stitch along both sides.

Machine stitch down the centre of the apron front to form the two pockets, finishing off with a triangle of stitches at the centre top to strengthen the stitching line. Remove all pins and basting stitches and press.

4 Make the waistband and ties by finding the centre of the strip of gabardine. Mark this point. Fold the strip in half lengthways and, with right sides together and matching the centre points, place the strip along the top edge of the apron front. Insert a pin at the edges of the apron and snip or mark the tie at these points.

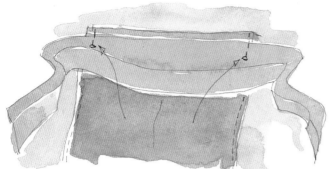

Remove the pins and fold the tie lengthways, with right sides together. Pin and baste, then, beginning at one of the short ends, machine stitch the tie together, turning at the corner and continuing up to the mark. Repeat at the other end.

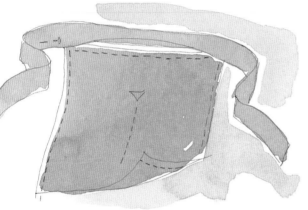

5 Clip the corners and turn the tie to the right side. Place it, right sides facing and matching centres, on the front of the apron so that the raw edges align. Pin and baste one side of the tie to the apron, then machine stitch in place. Remove pins and basting stitches and turn the tie to the back. Fold in the seam allowance and pin and baste in position before slip stitching to the back of the apron. Press before using your sewing-machine to top stitch the ties and waistband all round about ¼in/5mm from all edges.

SHELF EDGING

Finished size: 5¼ x 23in/13.5 x 58cm

This shelf edging is made entirely of felt and it has a scalloped edge and appliquéd leaf shapes. Since felt is non-woven it is ideal for appliqué because crisply cut shapes will not fray. This pretty blue and white design would be ideal in many situations.

Cut templates for the scallop and leaf shapes (see page 47). From the white felt cut two pieces, each 6 x 23in/15 x 58cm. From the blue felt cut one piece 6 x 23in/15 x 58cm and 16 leaf shapes.

YOU WILL NEED

- card for templates
- white felt: 9 x 72in/23 x 115cm
- blue felt: 9 x 72in/23 x 115cm
- needles, sewing thread, scissors, pins
- medium weight interfacing
- pinking shears

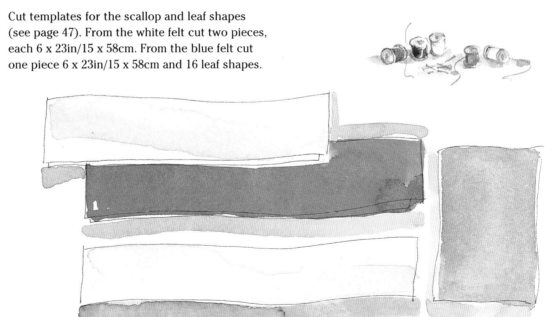

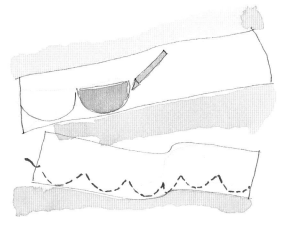

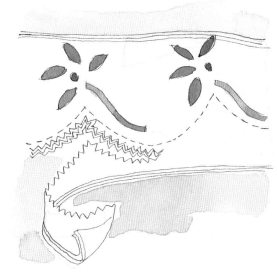

1 Place the scallop template about ⅜in/10mm from the bottom edge of one of the strips of white felt. Draw lightly around the template to make six shapes. Baste along this line.

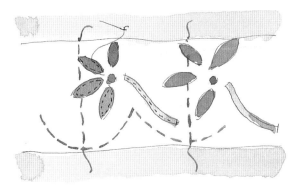

2 Mark and baste a vertical line through the centre of each shape. Using these lines as a guide, pin and tack the leaves to the white felt. Stitch in position with small running stitches. Cut narrow strips of blue felt, each ⅜ x 4in/ 8mm x 10cm, for the stems and carefully stitch them in position.

Cut small circles of blue felt and place them in the centre of each group of leaves. Stitch them in position. Remove the vertical lines of basting stitches.

3 Place the decorated felt strip on top of the second strip of white felt. Cut a strip of interfacing to fit and place it beneath the white felt. Pin, baste and stitch the three layers together on all edges, carefully stitching around the scallops on the drawn and basted lines. Remove the basting stitches.

Use pinking shears to cut carefully around the scallops, keeping ¼in/5mm from the stitched line.

4 Place the white felt on top of the blue felt, matching the scalloped edge to the bottom edge of the blue felt. Pin, baste and stitch around all the sides. Then carefully stitch around the scallops through all the layers. Trim the top edge if necessary before removing all tacking stitches.

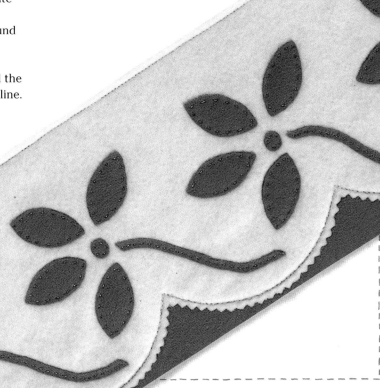

BOLSTER CUSHION

Finished size: about 22in/56cm long

The floral design has been applied to both ends of the bolster cushion using a technique known as appliqué perse *or Persian appliqué. This involves cutting out motifs from patterned fabric then reassembling them into a new design. We used a medium weight cotton fabric and machine stitched around each motif, but the cut-out shapes could be hand stitched in place, using a turned edge method throughout.*

Make a circular template, 7in/19cm in diameter, and draw around the template on one of the squares of background fabric. Baste around the drawn line. Repeat on the other square.

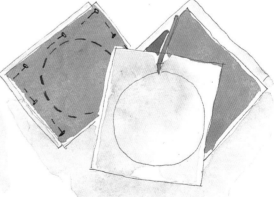

YOU WILL NEED

- card for template
- background fabric: 1 piece 18 x 23in/ 46 x 58cm; 2 pieces, each 10 x 10in/25 x 25cm
- needles, sewing thread to match, scissors, pins
- "stitch and tear" interfacing
- floral fabric (select a piece from which several motifs can be cut)
- zip fastener: 10in/25cm (optional)
- bolster cushion pad

1 Cut two squares of interfacing, each about 10 x 10in/25 x 25cm, and pin and baste them to the squares of background fabric.

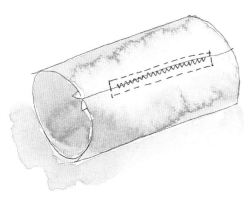

2 Cut out the chosen motifs from the patterned fabric, leaving a seam allowance of ¼in/5mm all round if they are to be attached by hand but slightly less than this if you are using a sewing-machine.

Arrange the motifs within the circles to make a pleasing pattern. If they are to be hand stitched, carefully clip around the edges of the motifs before turning them under so that they will lie flat. Pin, then baste them in position. Stitch around each motif. Press, remove the basting stitches and press again if necessary.

3 If a sewing-machine is used, pin and baste the motifs in position, then, with an even, dense satin stitch in a contrasting cotton, follow the outline of each shape. Remove the basting stitches and press.

4 Cut out the circles, leaving a seam allowance of ½in/10mm.

Take the rectangle of backing fabric and pin and baste the long sides together. Stitch, leaving a gap of 10in/25cm in the centre of the seam. Remove the basting stitches and press. Insert a zip fastener if wished.

5 With right sides facing, pin, baste and stitch the circles to the short ends of the tube. Clip around the seam and turn to the right side before pressing. Insert the cushion pad and close the gap in the long seam if a zip fastener has not been used.

TOY BAG

Finished size: 15 x 30in/37 x 75cm

We have used bright blue and red medium weight cotton, and matching plaid fabric, for this useful draw-string bag, which is decorated with black squirrels. The pieces are machine stitched, and the appliqué shapes are also machined on. The bag is lined, and the quilted base provides a firm foundation for a host of toys.

Trace the outline of the squirrels (see page 47) onto the interfacing, remembering that you need two pairs, facing in opposite directions. Do not remove the backing paper at this stage.

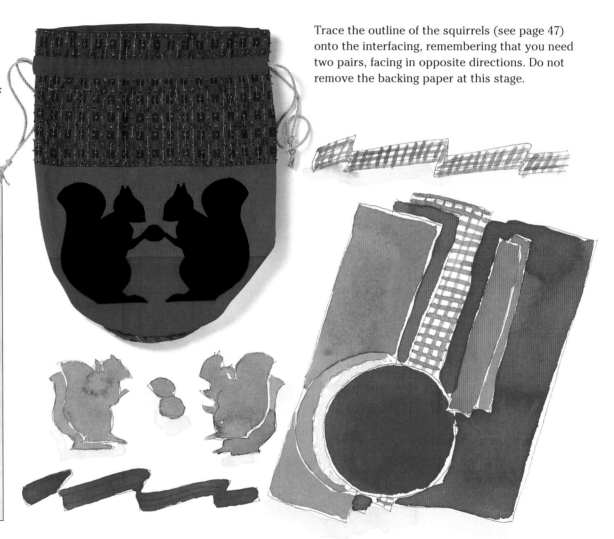

YOU WILL NEED

- card for templates
- fusible interfacing: 9 x 36in/23 x 90cm
- red fabric: 1 piece 5 x 30in/13 x 75cm; 1 piece 18 x 30in/46 x 75cm; 2 pieces, each 3 x 14in/7.5 x 36cm; 2 circles, each with a diameter of 9½in/24cm
- blue fabric: 1 piece 5 x 30in/13 x 75cm
- needles, sewing thread, scissors, pins
- plaid fabric: 1 piece 8 x 30in/20 x 75cm; 1 piece 1½ x 30in/4 x 75cm, cut on the bias (join 2 shorter pieces if necessary)
- black fabric: 9 x 36in/23 x 90cm
- freezer paper
- lightweight polyester wadding: 1 circle 9½in/24cm in diameter
- cord: 80in/2m

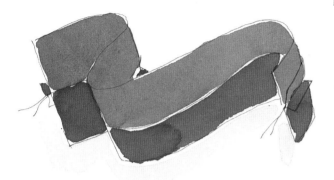

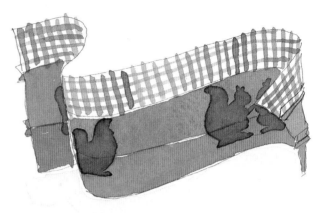

To keep the background smooth and wrinkle free while the motif is stitched in place, cut out a piece of freezer paper measuring about 8 x 8in/20 x 20cm and iron it onto the reverse side of the red and blue fabric, behind the squirrel.

Select a matching thread – we used black – and use your sewing-machine to satin stitch around the edge of the squirrel (see page 8). The stitches should be even and dense and completely cover all the raw edges. Fasten off on the reverse of the fabric and remove the freezer paper.

1 With right sides facing, pin and baste the red piece measuring 5 x 30in/13 x 75cm, and the blue piece measuring 5½ x 30in/14 x 75cm together. Stitch along one long edge, leaving a seam allowance of ½in/10mm. Remove the pins and basting stitches and press open the seam.

4 With the right sides together, pin and baste the plaid material to the top edge of the blue fabric. Stitch the pieces together, with a seam allowance of ½in/10mm. Remove the pins and basting stitches and press open the seam.

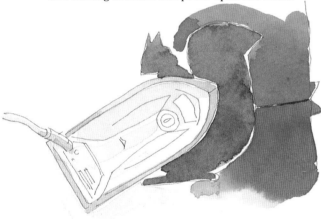

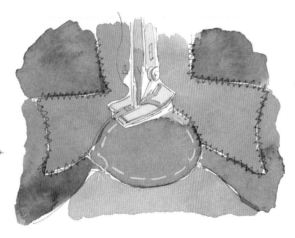

2 Cut roughly around the squirrels and iron the interfacing to the back of the black fabric. Carefully cut out the squirrels and place them, in pairs, on a flat surface.

Remove the backing paper from one squirrel and position it so that it covers the seam between the red and blue pieces and is approximately 2in/5cm from the side edge. Iron the squirrel in place.

3 Position the second motif so that it faces the first and aligns along the bottom edge. Leave a gap of about 1in/2.5cm between the front legs of the squirrels. Stitch the squirrel in position as before.

Cut out a nut shape from a piece of black fabric, bonded with interfacing, and stitch it between the two squirrels.

Position and stitch the remaining two squirrels on the red and blue fabric, placing the last one about 2in/5cm from the side edge.

5 Take the large piece of red fabric. This will be the lining of the bag so trim it to size if necessary. With right sides facing, pin and tack the long top edges together. Stitch, leaving a seam allowance of ½in/10mm, remove the pins and basting stitches and press the seam to one side.

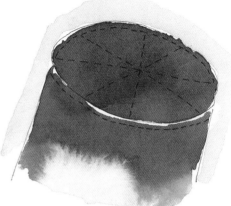

6 With the right sides facing, pin and baste the long side seam together to form one long tube. Stitch the seam, leaving an allowance of ½in/10mm, remove the pins and basting stitches and press open the seam.

7 Turn the bag the right way out and fold it along the seamed top edge. Align the side seams and pin and baste the bottom edges together. Top stitch around the top edge of the bag.

8 Take the two strips of red fabric and fold each in half lengthways. Stitch them to form a tube with a ¼in/5mm seam allowance. Press each tube so that the seam is in the centre. Turn in the ends and pin and baste each one to the top of the bag, about 1⅛in/4cm down from the top edge and with about 1⅛in/4cm between the strips. Top stitch along the top and bottom edges of the strips, leaving the ends open.

9 Use compasses to draw a circular template with a diameter of 9½in/24cm. Cut two red circles and one circle from the wadding. Fold one of the red circles into eighths and press it. Open out the circle and make a sandwich with the wadding in the centre. Pin and baste the three layers together. Stitch along the pressed creases to quilt the fabric. Remove all pins and basting stitches.

10 With the right sides facing, pin and baste the base to the bottom edge of the bag. Stitch around the bag so that the seam is on the outside. Remove the pins and basting stitches.

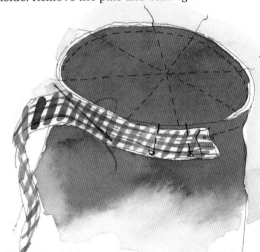

11 Take the long strip of plaid fabric. With right sides together and starting at the side seam, pin the bias strip to the bottom edge of the bag, leaving about ⅜in/10mm overlap at each end of the strip to be turned under to neaten. Stitch the bias strip to the base of the bag and remove all pins and basting stitches. Turn under about ¼in/5mm of the bias strip to neaten the raw edge and slip stitch it to the base of the bag.

12 Cut the cord into two equal lengths and thread each through the channels at the top of the bag in opposite directions. Knot the ends firmly together to stop the cord from fraying.

WALL-HANGING

Finished size: about 16 x 16in/40 x 40cm

This rainbow coloured fish is an appealing image for children of all ages, and it could be used as an aid to learning about colours. The fish is pieced together from strips of fabric, applied to the background material by the freezer paper technique, and it has been slightly padded to give a more rounded shape. The hanging is framed with a border of triangles, and the edges have been bound with a dark patterned fabric. Medium weight fabric has been used throughout.

Make a template for the fish's body (see page 48). From both the lavender and violet fabrics cut a piece measuring 4 x 7in/10 x 19cm. From each of the other coloured fabrics cut one piece measuring 1½ x 7in/4 x 19cm.

YOU WILL NEED

- card for template
- red, orange, yellow, green, blue, indigo, violet and lavender fabrics: about 9 x 45in/ 23 x 115cm of each colour
- needles, sewing thread, scissors, pins
- freezer paper
- background fabric: 18 x 45in/46 x 115cm
- button toy eye or small circle of felt
- small amount of polyester toy stuffing
- calico: 18 x 45in/46 x 115cm
- lightweight polyester wadding
- binding fabric: 9 x 45in/23 x 115cm
- ½in/10mm dowel, 18in/46cm long

1 With seam allowances of ¼in/5mm on all pieces, stitch the rectangles together in the following order: lavender, red, orange, yellow, green, blue, indigo and violet. Press all seams to one side.

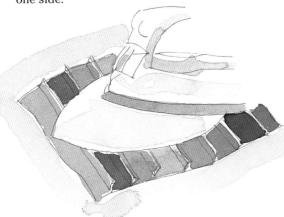

2 Reverse the fish template and draw around the outline on the paper side of the freezer paper. Cut out the shape and iron it to the wrong side of the coloured fabrics. Cut out around the fish shape, allowing ½in/10mm all round, and clip into the curves by about ¼in/5mm. Press the seam allowance down over the freezer paper.

3 Cut a square of background fabric measuring 12½ x 12½in/32 x 32cm and position the fish on the square. Pin and baste. Slip stitch around the fish shape, leaving a gap of about 2in/5cm in the centre of the top edge. Remove pins and basting. Carefully remove the freezer paper through the gap, then use a small amount of polyester stuffing to pad the shape. Slip stitch to close the gap.

Follow the manufacturer's instructions to assemble and attach the eye or, if the hanging is for a small child, use a small circle of felt, firmly stitched in place.

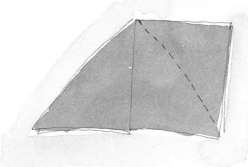

4 From the lavender fabric, cut a square 2 x 2in/5 x 5cm and fold it in half. Press the folded corners in towards the centre to form a triangle and press. Attach to the fish by stitching through the apex of the triangle, to form a tail.

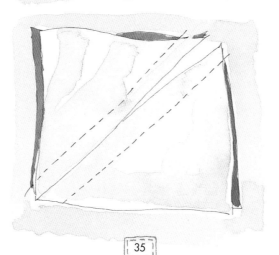

5 Cut 14 squares, each 4 x 4in/10 x 10cm, from the calico, and on each square draw a diagonal line, then draw a line ¼in/5mm on each side of the diagonal line.

From each colour, except lavender, cut two squares, each 4 x 4in/10 x 10cm. Place a calico square on a coloured square and stitch them together along the two lines on either side of the diagonal line. Cut through both layers along the central, diagonal line and press the seams to one side, thus making two squares, half-calico, half-colour.

6 Make 28 squares in this way, then pin a row together in the following sequence: red, orange, yellow, green, blue and indigo. Baste then stitch the squares together with a ¼in/5mm seam allowance. Make another strip to match. Pin and baste one strip to the top of the square of backing fabric. Repeat at the bottom, then stitch both strips in place.

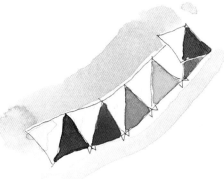

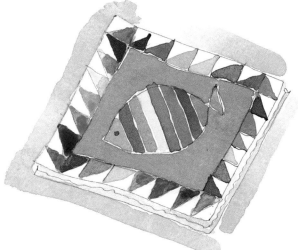

8 Trim the wadding to fit and cut a square of backing fabric to match the dimensions of the finished front section. Place the three layers together and baste, running stitches in a grid to hold the pieces securely together.

7 Make two more strips from the remaining half-calico, half-colour squares, arranging the colours in the following sequence: violet, red, orange, yellow, green, blue, indigo, violet. Turn the first violet square through 180 degrees to join it to the red triangle. Pin, baste then stitch these strips to the sides of the backing square, taking care that the corner seams align. Press.

9 From the binding fabric cut four strips, each 2½ x 17in/6 x 43cm. Fold in half lengthways with wrong sides together and press. With raw edges aligned and right sides facing, pin and baste a binding strip to the top and bottom edges. Stitch, then turn to wrong side, turn in the ends to neaten, and slip stitch down. Repeat on the two side edges, neatening the corners with overstitches. Slip stitch to wrong side.

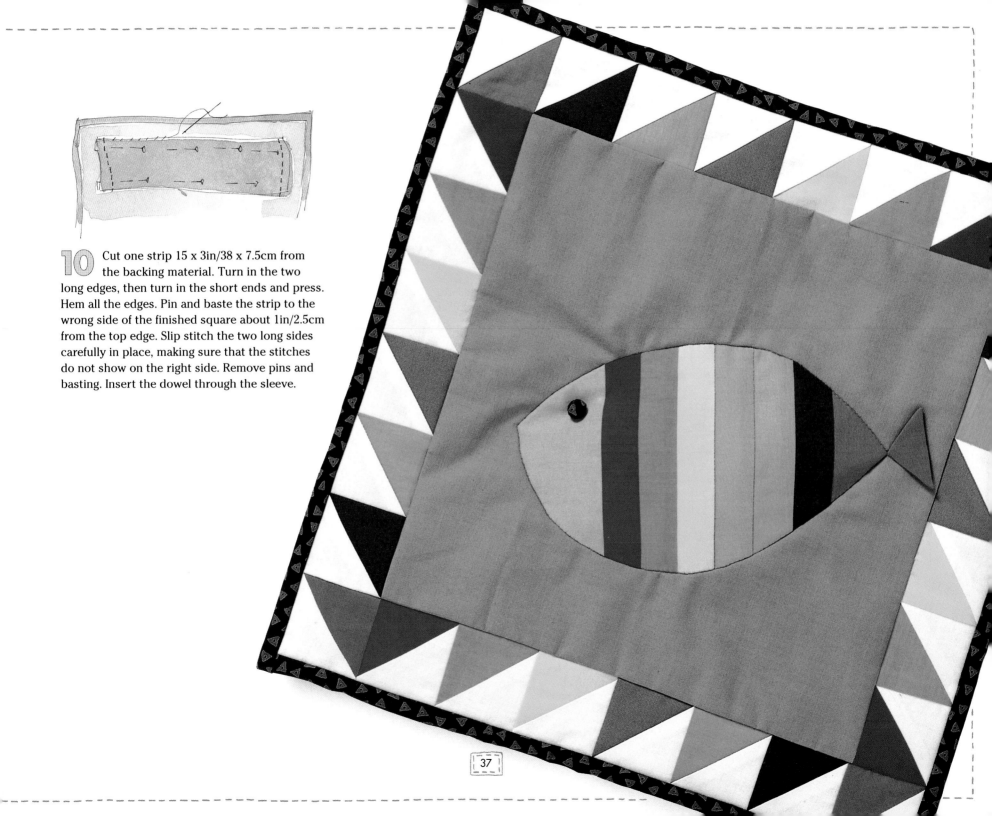

10 Cut one strip 15 x 3in/38 x 7.5cm from the backing material. Turn in the two long edges, then turn in the short ends and press. Hem all the edges. Pin and baste the strip to the wrong side of the finished square about 1in/2.5cm from the top edge. Slip stitch the two long sides carefully in place, making sure that the stitches do not show on the right side. Remove pins and basting. Insert the dowel through the sleeve.

PILLOWCASE WITH RIBBON APPLIQUÉ

Finished size: 26 x 21in/66 x 53cm

The crisp broderie anglaise is hand stitched *to the pillowcase in a simple diamond shape. Ribbon is used for a trim and tiny bows have been added to complete the design. The ribbon can be chosen to suit the colour of the decor, while the crisp white pillowcase and broderie anglaise would make this a perfect wedding or christening gift.*

Choose an appropriate design of broderie anglaise for your purpose and complement it with contrasting ribbon.

YOU WILL NEED

- 1 white pillowcase
- quilter's masking tape, ¼in/5mm wide
- cardboard
- needles, sewing thread to match, scissors, pins
- broderie anglaise, 3in/7.5cm wide (with a raw edge): 2yd/1.8m
- ribbon, ½in/10mm wide: 2yd/1.8m
- ribbon, ⅛in/3mm wide: 1yd/90cm

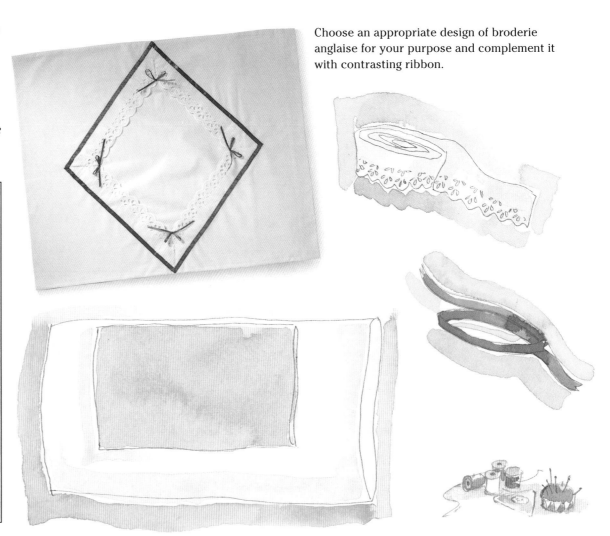

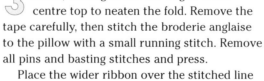

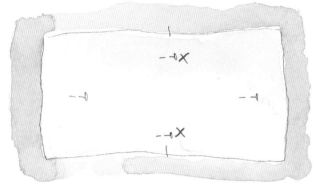

1 Place the pillowcase on a flat surface. Measure and use masking tape to mark a horizontal line across the centre of the pillowcase. Insert a piece of cardboard inside the pillowcase so that your stitches do not go through both layers. Place a pin about 4in/10cm in from each side edge and mark the central points of both long edges.

3 Baste, turning in the raw edges at the centre top to neaten the fold. Remove the tape carefully, then stitch the broderie anglaise to the pillow with a small running stitch. Remove all pins and basting stitches and press.

Place the wider ribbon over the stitched line and stitch in place, folding carefully into neat mitred angles at the corners.

4 Make four small ribbon bows and stitch them in position at the points of the diamond. Remove the cardboard.

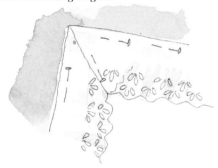

2 Placing the broderie anglaise, edge facing inwards, make a diamond shape with one complete length. Begin at the centre of the top edge and pin the broderie anglaise in a straight line to the point marked by the pin on the left side of the centre line.

Turn the broderie anglaise with a mitre fold on the wrong side and continue to pin, diagonally, in a straight line to the centre point on the bottom edge. Repeat to complete the diamond.

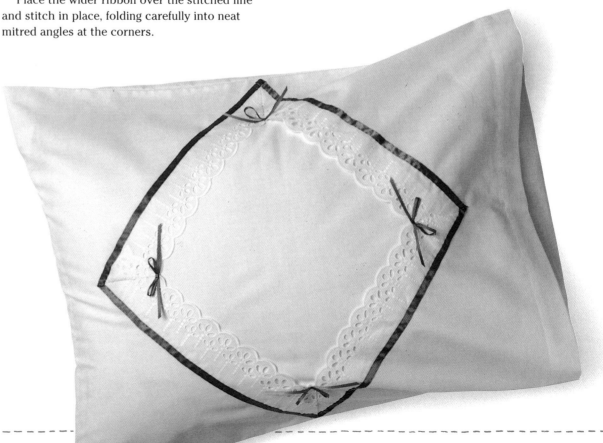

CHRISTMAS RING IN SHADOW APPLIQUÉ

Finished size: 12in/30cm in diameter

You will be able to use this pretty ring as a
Christmas decoration for years to come.
The parcel and holly motifs are cut from
brightly coloured fabrics, which are placed on
a white background, and these are overlaid
with a layer of fine voile to give a softer,
subtler effect. Hand stitching around the
shapes traps them between the background
fabric and the voile, and a tartan ribbon and
bow add the perfect finishing touches.

From both the voile and the white fabric cut a
square 14 x 14in/36 x 36cm.

Cut templates for the bow and the holly leaves
(see page 48). From the red fabric cut one square
4½ x 4½in/11.5 x 11.5cm and four small circles.
From the green fabric cut four holly leaves. From
the patterned fabric cut one bow.

YOU WILL NEED

- voile, organza or fine muslin: 18 x 45in/
  46 x 115cm
- white background fabric: 18 x 45in/
  46 x 115cm
- card for templates
- scraps of red, green and patterned fabrics
- circular embroidery frame, 10in/25cm in
  diameter
- glue stick
- needles, sewing thread, scissors, pins
- pinking shears
- tartan ribbon, 1in/2.5cm wide: 2yd/1.8m
- green ribbon, ½in/10mm wide: 2yd/1.8m
- small brass pins

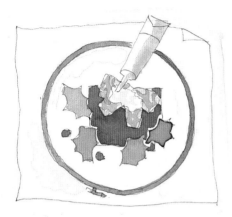

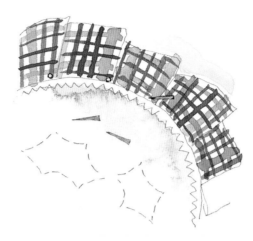

1 Place the embroidery frame on the white fabric and arrange the coloured shapes within the circle. When you are satisfied with the arrangement, use a spot of adhesive to hold the shapes in place.

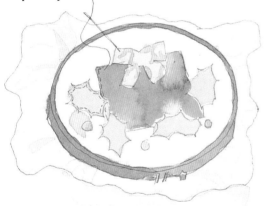

2 Lift away the embroidery frame and cover the shapes with voile. Place both layers of material in the embroidery frame and tighten it to hold the fabric tightly. The screw should be at the bottom of the design.

Use white sewing thread to work a small running stitch around all the shapes. The stitches should be no more than ⅛in/3mm from the edge of the shapes.

3 Trim the surplus fabric close to the edge of the ring with pinking shears.

Pleat and pin the tartan ribbon to the wrong side of the ring, overlapping it to conceal the raw edges at the bottom of the ring.

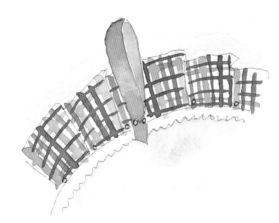

4 Glue green ribbon to the side of the ring. Trim off the surplus ribbon.

Make a small loop of green ribbon and pin it to the top of the ring.

5 Cut a length of green ribbon 10in/25cm long and fold the ends together at the centre. Stitch in place.

Cut a length of green ribbon 12in/30cm long and fold it in half over the loop made in the previous step. Stitch it to the centre of the loop. Place the bow at the centre bottom of the frame and use very small stitches to attach it to the fabric.

EARRING PILLOW

Finished size: 6½ x 6½in/18 x 18cm

Keep your earrings safe and in pairs by arranging them neatly on this small pillow. The cream calico will complement any colour scheme, and the reverse appliqué centre is enhanced by the rich burgundy red. The edges of the open appliqué shapes have been neatened with simple overstitching.

YOU WILL NEED

- needles, sewing thread to match, scissors, pins
- calico: 1 square 7 x 7in/19 x 19cm; 1 square 2½ x 2½in/6 x 6cm; 1 strip 1¾in/4.5cm wide and about 1yd/90cm long
- red fabric: 2½ x 2½in/6 x 6cm
- cream pearl cotton (coton perlé)
- polyester wadding or fine, clean sawdust

Place a ruler diagonally across the small calico square and, starting ¼in/5mm from one corner, draw a line 1in/2.5cm long. Repeat from the other three corners.

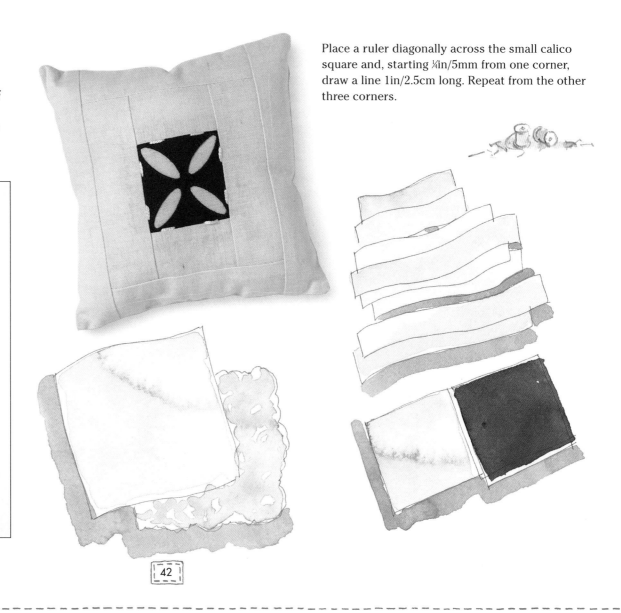

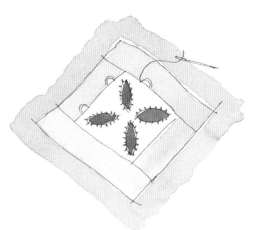

1 Use a small pair of sharp-pointed scissors to cut along each line to make a slit. Place this square on top of the red square. Pin and baste all four edges together.

2 Carefully fold under the cut edges of each slit to reveal the red fabric below. Use a needle or the point of a scissor blade to encourage the fabric to turn under.

Oversew around the edges of each shape, making several stitches at the ends of each oval and making sure that the stitches go through both layers of fabric.

3 Cut a strip 1¾ x 2½in/4.5 x 6cm and place it, right sides facing and with raw edges aligned, along one side of the centre square. Pin and baste, then stitch the two pieces together, with a seam allowance of ¼in/5mm.

Repeat at the opposite side, then press the seams together and outwards. Take another strip, 1¾in/4.5cm wide and about 5in/13cm long, and place it along one of the other sides, right sides together. Pin and baste, then stitch the pieces together, stitching across the short end strips as well as along the centre square. Repeat at the other side so that the centre square is framed by the four strips. Press the seams together and outwards.

4 Use pearl cotton to make two loops along each of the four seams, positioning them evenly along the sides of the central square.

5 Add four more strips around the edge in the same way as before – that is, adding strips to two opposite sides before adding the longer strips on the two remaining sides. Press all seams outwards. With right sides facing, pin and baste the finished square to the large square of calico.

6 Stitch around all the sides, with a seam
allowance of ¼in/5mm, and leave an
opening of about 2in/5cm in the centre of one
side. Trim the corners and turn the pillow to the
right side, using the blunt end of a knitting
needle or something similar to push the corners
out. Press again.
    Fill the pillow firmly with polyester wadding
or sawdust before neatly oversewing the
opening.

TEMPLATES

HAWAIIAN APPLIQUÉ CUSHION PAGE 12
actual size, including ¼in/5mm seam allowance

grain of fabric

fold

fold

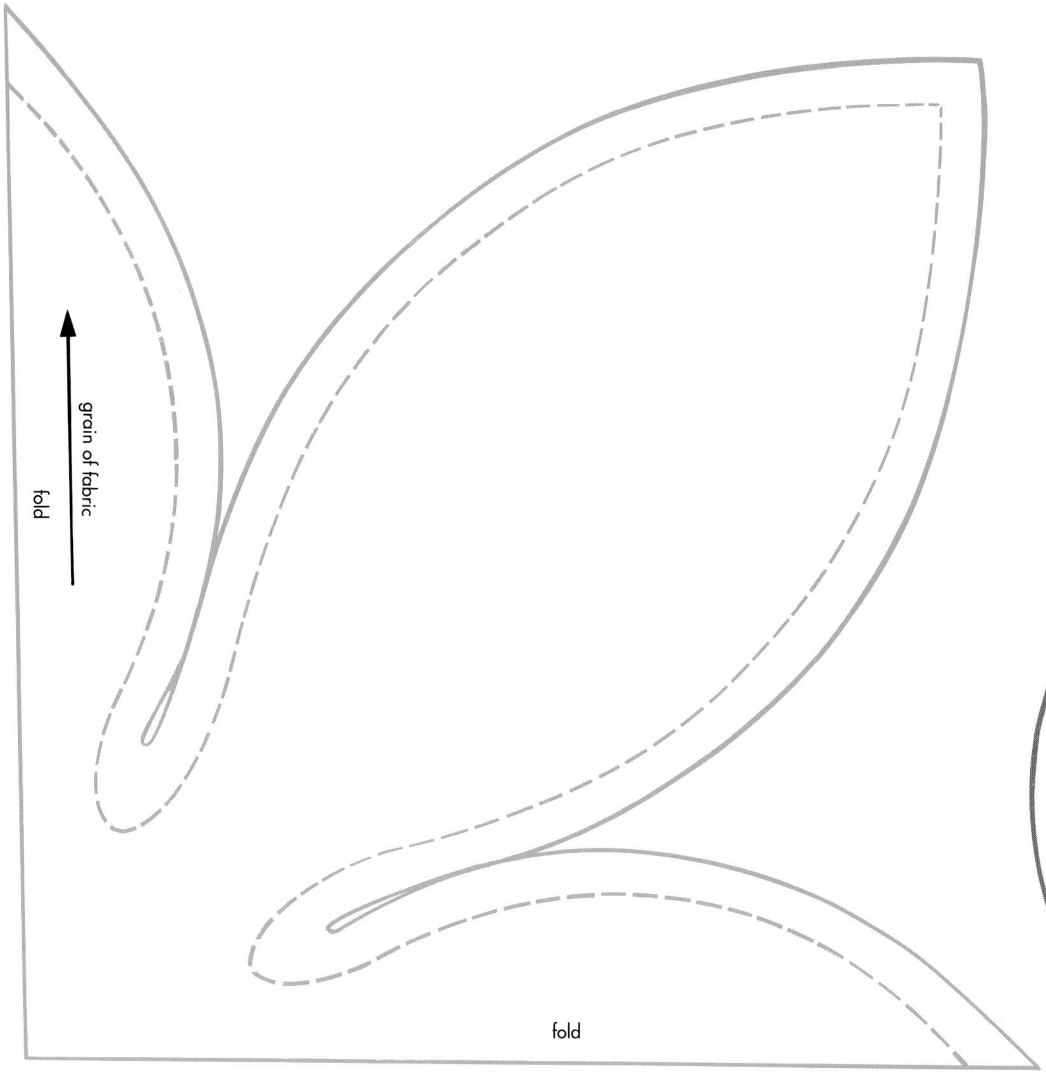

STAR PAN HOLDER PAGE 15
A TEMPLATE FOR FABRIC   B TEMPLATE FOR PAPER
actual size, including ¼in/5mm seam allowance

top

grain of fabric

A

B

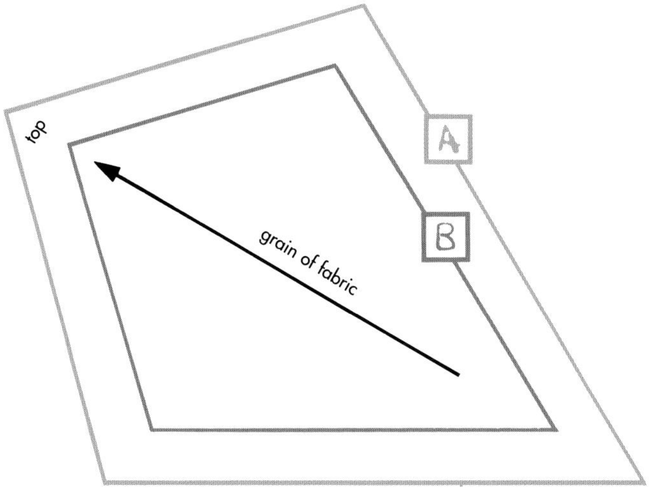

TABLE MAT PAGE 18
A APPLE B LEAF
actual size, no seam allowance

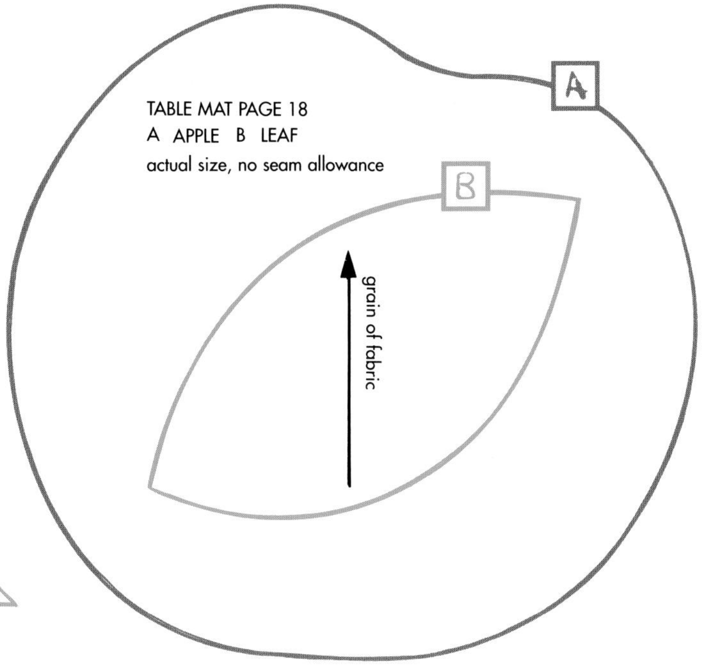

grain of fabric

A

B

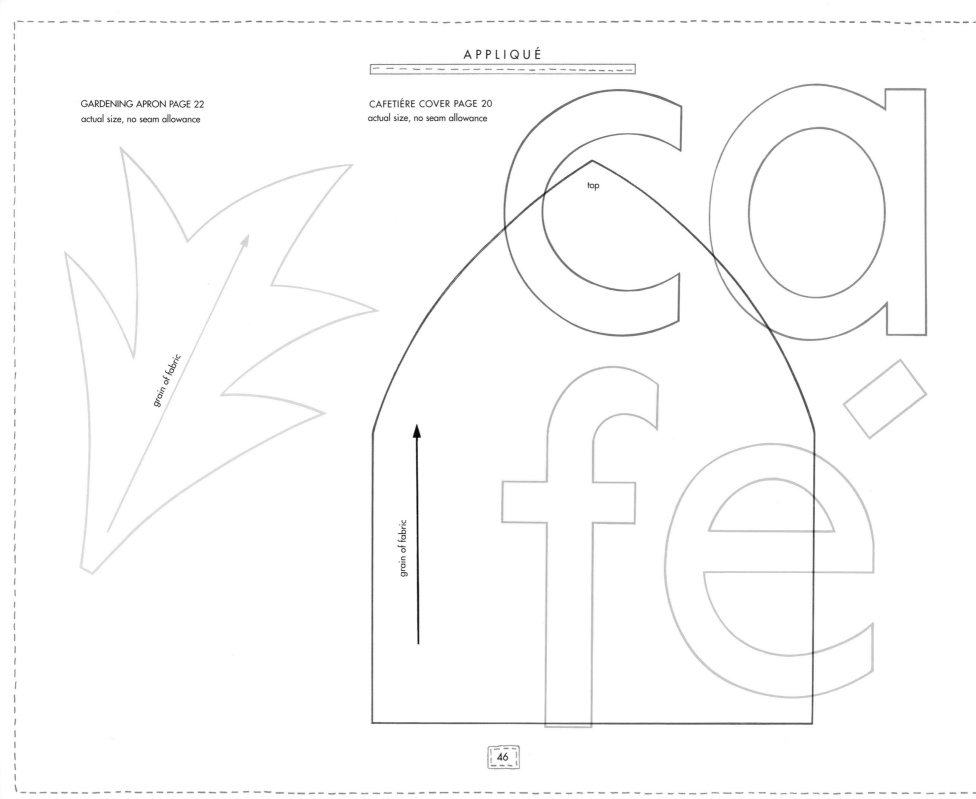

APPLIQUÉ

GARDENING APRON PAGE 22
actual size, no seam allowance

CAFETIÈRE COVER PAGE 20
actual size, no seam allowance

grain of fabric

top

grain of fabric

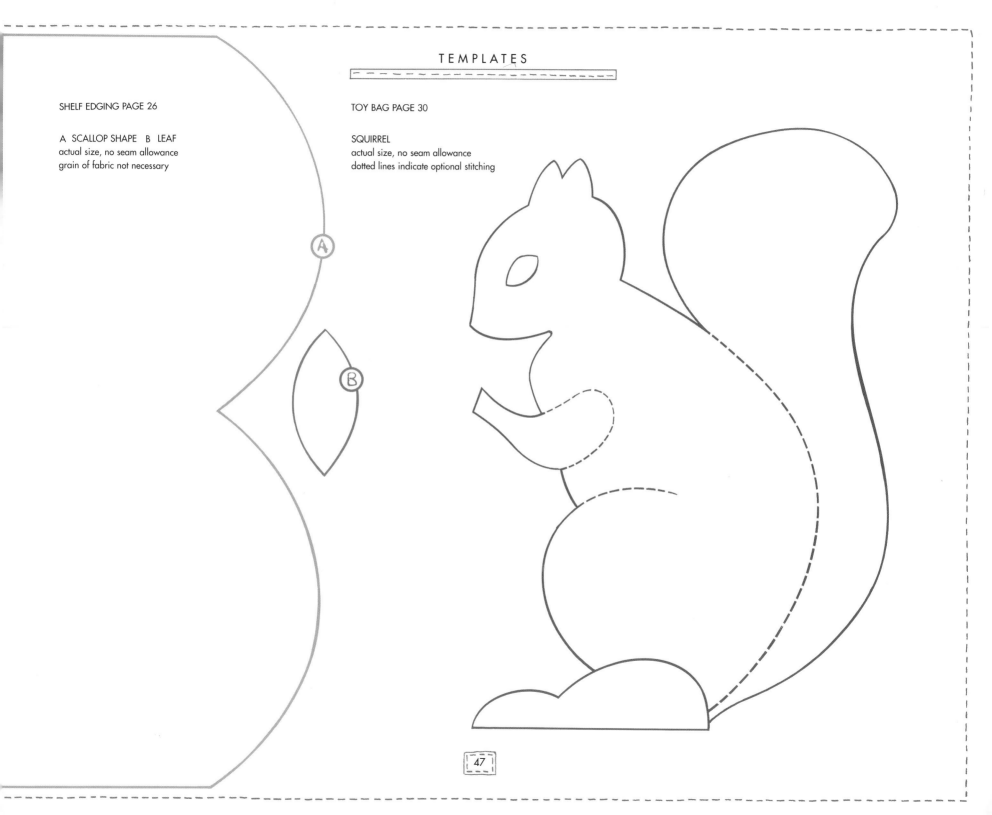

TEMPLATES

SHELF EDGING PAGE 26

A SCALLOP SHAPE   B LEAF
actual size, no seam allowance
grain of fabric not necessary

Ⓐ

Ⓑ

TOY BAG PAGE 30

SQUIRREL
actual size, no seam allowance
dotted lines indicate optional stitching

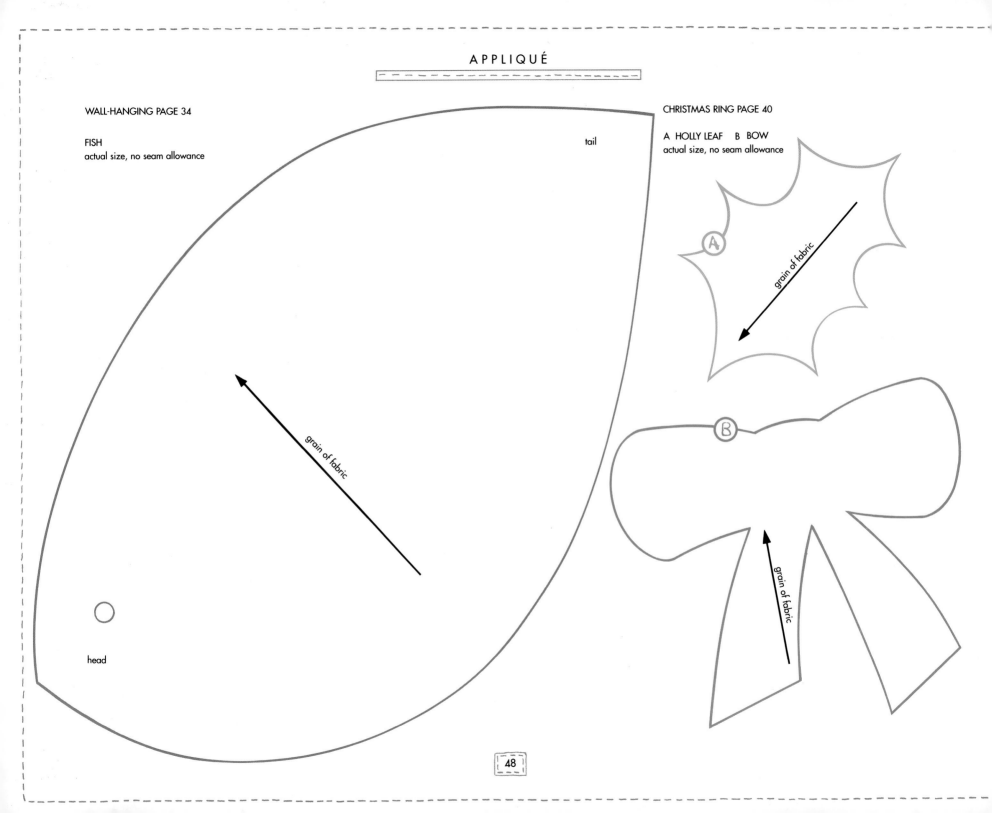

APPLIQUÉ

WALL-HANGING PAGE 34

FISH
actual size, no seam allowance

tail

grain of fabric

head

CHRISTMAS RING PAGE 40

A HOLLY LEAF   B BOW
actual size, no seam allowance

Ⓐ

grain of fabric

Ⓑ

grain of fabric